W9-CFC-598

Food from Farmers

FRUIT!

Life on a Apple Farm

by Ruth Owen

WINDMILL BOOKS

New York

Published in 2012 by Windmill Books, an Imprint of Rosen Publishing
29 East 21st Street, New York, NY 10010

Editor for Ruby Tuesday Books Ltd: Mark J. Sachner
U.S. Editor: Julia Quinlan
Designer: Emma Randall
Consultant: Logan Peterman, Laughing Sprout Family Farm

Photo Credits: Cover, 1, 4–5, 6–7, 8–9, 10–11, 12 (top), 13 (bottom), 14–15, 16–17, 18–19, 20–21, 22–23, 24, 25 (bottom), 26–27, 28–29, 30–31 © Shutterstock; 12 (bottom) © Wikipedia (Creative Commons public domain); 13 (top) © FLPA; 25 (top) © Superstock.

Library of Congress Cataloging-in-Publication Data

Owen, Ruth, 1967–
Fruit! : life on an apple farm / by Ruth Owen.
p. cm. — (Food from farmers)
Includes index.
ISBN 978-1-61533-530-5 (library binding) — ISBN 978-1-61533-538-1 (pbk.) —
ISBN 978-1-61533-539-8 (6-pack)
1. Apples—Juvenile literature. 2. Farm life—Juvenile literature. I. Title. II. Title: Life on an apple farm. III. Series: Food from farmers.
SB363.O94 2012
634'.11—dc23

2011026648

Manufactured in the United States of America

CPSIA Compliance Information: Batch #BOW2102WM: For Further Information contact Windmill Books, New York, New York at 1-866-478-0556

CONTENTS

WELCOME TO MY FARM!

Hi! My name is Hannah. I am 12 years old. I live on a farm with my mom and grandparents. Our farm grows apples.

An apple farm is known as an **orchard**. People have been growing apples for thousands of years!

I'm the fourth **generation** of our family to live on this apple farm. My great-grandfather started the farm. My grandfather grew up here, so did my mom!

Our farm is in the state of Washington. Washington produces more apples than any other U.S. state. If all the apples grown here in a year were laid side-by-side, they could circle the Earth 29 times!

My favorite type of apple is Red Delicious.

RED'S ORCHARD FACTS

- There are 7,500 apple orchards in the United States growing 100 different types of apples.

LET'S LOOK AROUND THE FARM

This is a map of our farm. Grandma and Grandpa live in the farmhouse. Mom and I live in the cottage.

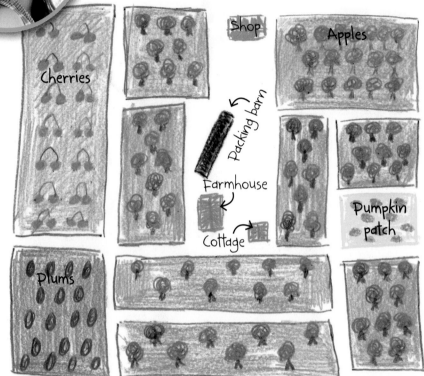

Cherries

Shop

Apples

Packing barn

Farmhouse

Cottage

Plums

Pumpkin patch

The farm covers 60 **acres** (28 hectares) of land.

There are thousands of apple trees on the farm. The trees are planted in rows.

RED'S ORCHARD FACTS

- An acre is a measurement used to measure farms.
- An acre is just a little smaller than a football field.
- An acre equals 0.4 hectare.

Mom and Grandpa work on the farm.
There are ten other workers, too.

We grow six different types of apples.
We grow Red Delicious, Golden Delicious,
Granny Smith, Fuji, Gala, and Braeburn.

Golden Delicious

Granny Smith

Gala

We also have cherry and
plum trees.

This is the pumpkin patch.
At Halloween we sell hundreds
of pumpkins!

Cherries

THE LIFE CYCLE OF AN APPLE TREE

Let's find out how an apple tree produces seeds and fruit!

In spring, an apple tree produces flowers called apple blossoms.

Bee

Honeybees visit the apple blossoms and **pollinate** the flowers. We'll find out more about pollination on the next page.

Once the apple blossoms are pollinated, they start to produce seeds.
The blossoms fall from the tree. On the tree, beneath each blossom, is a tiny apple. The seeds are in here.

The apples grow bigger.

Tiny apple

In autumn the apples fall from the tree. If the apples are left on the ground, the flesh will rot away. Now, the seeds inside each apple are on the ground. Some of the seeds may grow into new apple trees!

RED'S APPLE FACTS

- **An apple may contain up to 12 seeds.**

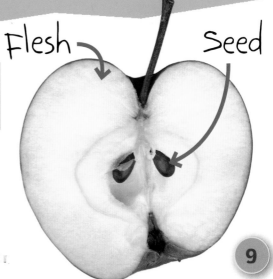

Flesh

Seed

FARMERS NEED BEES!

Bees are very important for producing food. If we didn't have bees, we wouldn't have apples and other fruits and vegetables!

Before an apple tree can make seeds and apples, it must be pollinated.

Yellow dust, called **pollen**, must be collected from the male part of a blossom on one apple tree. Then the pollen must be carried to the female part of a blossom on another tree.

Honeybees do this important job!

A honeybee lands on an apple blossom and walks around. The pollen sticks to its furry body.

Then the bee flies to a blossom on another tree. The pollen on the bee's body gets left on the female part of that blossom. Now the blossom is pollinated and can make seeds and apples!

Pollen

RED'S HONEYBEE FACTS

- Flowers get honeybees to visit them by producing a sweet liquid, called nectar, that the bees eat.

MAKING APPLE TREES

Every person or animal is slightly different. The same is true of apple seeds. Every seed will grow into a tree that is slightly different than its parent tree.

On the farm, we need to be sure what type of apple tree we are growing. If we want to sell Red Delicious apples, we must grow Red Delicious trees.

Net to protect trees from hail

Red Delicious trees

A seed from a Red Delicious apple might not grow into a Red Delicious tree. So, apple farmers have a clever way of making the type of tree we want.

First, Grandpa plants a small young tree. This is called rootstock. It is just a stem and some roots.

Red Delicious twig

Then, Grandpa takes a twig from a Red Delicious tree. The twig is slotted into the rootstock. Now the twig will join to the rootstock and grow into a Red Delicious tree!

Rootstock

Young trees

RED'S APPLE TREE FACTS

- **The young tree will be planted in the orchard when it is about two years old.**

13

A YEAR ON AN APPLE FARM

Life on an apple farm is always busy.

WINTER

It's cold and the trees are taking a rest.

In winter, the trees' old branches are pruned, or cut off. This lets more sunlight and air onto the trees to keep them healthy.

SPRING

New young apple trees are planted in the orchards.

Bees

When the apple blossoms appear, the trees need honeybees. Jo and Carl are **beekeepers**. They bring their honeybees to the orchard in their hives.

The bees live in the hives.

RED'S ORCHARD FACTS

- **Apple orchards have systems of long pipes and sprinklers to deliver water to the trees.**

SUMMER The apples are as big as golf balls.

Any apples that are a funny shape or not healthy are taken off the tree. Now, the best apples can use all the tree's energy to grow bigger.

Unhealthy apple

IT'S HARVEST TIME!

By August, the apples are **ripe**. This means they are fully grown and just right for picking and eating. It's **harvest** time!

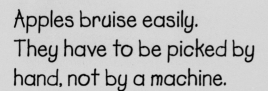

Apples bruise easily. They have to be picked by hand, not by a machine.

The apple pickers use ladders to reach the fruit.

The pickers wear cloth collection buckets over their shoulders.

The apples are emptied from the buckets into large wooden bins.

RED'S HARVEST FACTS

• **Each apple bin holds about 900 pounds (408 kg) of apples!**

Some of the apples go into a giant refrigerator in our packing barn.

The rest of the bins of apples are loaded onto a truck.
They are on their way to a large fruit company.

AT THE APPLE-PACKING PLANT

Our apples arrive at the fruit company's packing plant.

Machines sort the apples by color, weight, and **quality**. The apples are sent to big water tanks called flumes.

The apples are gently washed to remove any dirt.

Flume →

Apples have a thin layer of **wax** on their skins.
This keeps the juice inside the apple from drying up.
Washing the apples removes the wax.
At the plant, a machine sprays a new layer of wax onto the apples.
The wax is made from plants.

Trays

Carton

A machine puts a sticker on each apple.
Then they are put in trays and packed in cartons.
Now they are ready to go to stores and supermarkets.

RED'S APPLE FACTS

• **Apples don't grow all year round, but storing them in special cold warehouses keeps them fresh enough to eat for up to a year!**

PICK YOUR OWN!

At harvest time, customers can come to our farm and pick apples.

This is called "pick your own" or "U-pick."

The customers choose which type of apple they want to buy. They then pick the apples themselves. The apples are weighed, and the customers pay for what they have picked.

Sometimes Grandpa gives rides around the orchards. People ride in a trailer on the back of the tractor. Grandpa tells the visitors all about being an apple farmer.

Grandma bakes lots of apple pies. On Saturdays, I help Grandma sell slices of pie to the visitors.

Apple cider

Apple pie

Picking your own apples is a fun day out!

APPLES FOR SALE!

Apple farmers sell their apples in lots of different ways!

Some apples are sold in supermarkets and other food stores.

Some are sold to factories that make foods such as applesauce, apple juice, apple pies, apple chips, and cider.

Mom and Grandma sell some of our apples in our farm shop.
The shop sells other foods produced by local farmers, too.
We sell honey, vegetables, jam, and Grandma's frozen apple pies.

On Saturdays in the fall, we have a stand at a farmers' market. At the market, local farmers sell foods such as meat, fruit, vegetables, cheese, and bread.

RED'S APPLE FACTS

- About four out of every 10 apples grown in the United States are used in apple foods.

I help set out the fruit at the market.

TIME FOR SOME DELICIOUS CIDER!

We make sweet cider from our apples to sell in the shop.

Apple cider is made from freshly squeezed apples. It has no sugar added to it or chemicals to keep it fresh.

The apples are washed and cut into pieces. They are put into a machine called an apple grinder. The grinder is a little like a big food blender. The grinder crushes the apples into apple mash.

RED'S APPLE FACTS

- It takes about 35 to 40 apples to make one gallon (4 liters) of cider.

Cider press

Apple mash in cloth

This is Michael. He works on the farm.

Cider

The apple mash is laid on cloth on wooden trays.
The trays are stacked on top of each other in the cider press.
The cider press pushes down on the layers of trays.
The juice is squeezed from the mash.

The delicious fresh cider is put into bottles.

A DAY IN THE LIFE OF A FARM

Apple farmers work very hard!

7:00 a.m.
Grandpa mows the grass beneath the trees in the orchard.

8:00 a.m.
Some of the water sprinklers are not working right. It's hot, and the apple trees need water. Grandpa fixes the sprinklers.

9:00 a.m.
The apple pickers are hard at work. Mom washes and packs apples in the barn.

RED'S APPLE FACTS

- **At harvest time in Washington, about 45,000 people are at work picking apples!**

11:00 a.m.
Mom delivers boxes of apples to local stores in the truck.

1:00 p.m.
Mom serves customers in our shop.

3:00 p.m.
Mom and Grandpa pick apples.
I help when I get home from school.

6:00 p.m.
Mom packs the truck with fruit. Tomorrow is market day, and we need to set off at 6:00 a.m!

7:00 p.m.
Time for supper. Pork chops and apple coleslaw!

WE LOVE APPLES!

Apples taste great, and they are very good for our bodies.

There's an old saying: "An apple a day keeps the doctor away." It turns out that apples really do help keep us healthy!

Eating apples helps keep your heart working well.

Apples contain substances called **antioxidants**. These substances help protect our bodies against cancer.

Apples contain lots of **fiber**. Fiber keeps your **digestive system** working well.

28

RED'S APPLE FACTS

- **Don't peel your apples. The peel contains lots of fiber and antioxidants.**

Everyone should eat at least two servings of fruit and three servings of vegetables every day. These are my favorite ways to get my daily fruit goodness.

A crunchy apple as a snack.

Applesauce or pancakes filled with grated apple.

Thank you to apple farmers everywhere!

GLOSSARY

acre (AY-ker)
A unit of measurement used for measuring land, especially on farms.

antioxidants (an-tee-OK-suh-dunts)
Substances found in fruits and vegetables that keep our bodies healthy.

beekeeper (BEE-kee-pur)
A person who keeps and cares for large colonies, or groups, of bees. The bees live in homes called hives. When the bees make honey, the beekeeper collects it to sell.

digestive system (dy-JES-tiv SIS-tem)
The group of body parts, such as the stomach, that break down food so that a body can use it for fuel.

fiber (FY-ber)
Material found in plants. Your body can't break down fiber, so it pushes it through your digestive system, which helps keep your poop moving out of your body.

generation (jeh-nuh-RAY-shun)
The different ages, or layers, of a family. You are one generation, your parents

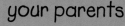

are an earlier generation, and your grandparents are the generation that came before that.

harvest (HAR-vist)
The time of year when fruits, vegetables, and other crops, such as wheat or corn, are ready to be picked or collected for eating and selling.

orchard (OR-cherd)
A farm that grows fruit, or the area on a farm where fruit trees are planted.

pollen (PAH-lin)
A yellow dust produced by the male part of a flower called the anther.

pollinate (PAH-luh-nayt)
To move pollen from one flower to another so that the plant can reproduce (make more plants) by making seeds.

quality (KWAH-luh-tee)
How good something is. An apple's quality may be judged on its shape, its freshness, or its taste.

ripe (RYP)
Fully grown and ready to be eaten.

wax (WAKS)
A greasy substance that can come from animal bodies or plants. Your ears make earwax!

WEB SITES
For Web resources related to the subject of this book, go to: www.windmillbooks.com/weblinks and select this book's title.

READ MORE

Ward, Kristin. *Apples. Nature Books.* New York: PowerKids Press, 2000.
Hewitt, Sally. *Fruit. Good for Me.* New York: PowerKids Press, 2008.
Maestro, Betsy. *How Do Apples Grow?* New York: Harper Collins, 1992.

INDEX